Famous Female
Authors

VERONICA ROTH

Author of the
DIVERGENT TRILOGY

by Lori Mortensen

Snap books®

CAPSTONE PRESS
a capstone imprint

Snap Books are published by Capstone Press
1710 Roe Crest Drive, North Mankato, Minnesota 56003
www.mycapstone.com

Cataloging-in-Publication Data is on file with the Library of Congress.
ISBN 978-1-5157-1327-2 (library binding)
ISBN 978-1-5157-1335-7 (paperback)
ISBN 978-1-5157-1339-5 (eBook PDF)

Editorial Credits
Abby Colich, editor; Bobbi J. Wyss, designer;
Kelly Garvin, media researcher; Laura Manthe, production specialist

Photo Credits
Alamy: CBW, 7 (bottom inset), Steve Skjold, 11, Zuma Press Inc, 19; AP Images/Scott
Eisen, 5; Getty Images: John Lamparski/WireImage, 23, Lily Lawrence/WireImage, 28;
Newscom: AIAA/ZDS WENN Photos, 27, Mark Doyle/Splash News, 21; Shutterstock: 89
studio, 5, 18, 23 (b), 29, Ditty_about_summer, 9, Eugene Moerman, 14, Jaguar PS,
25, Kirill Smirnov, cover, 1, Melkor3D, 13, Natali Zakharova, 20, Pixsooz, 17, Richard
Cavalleri, 7, Tursunbaev Ruslan, cover, 1, Zlatko Guzmic, cover (bottom), 1

Printed in China.
007736

TABLE OF CONTENTS

CHAPTER 1

Marshmallow Madness

For eight months Veronica Roth had been filling her blog with the ups and downs of her life as a writer. On March 31, 2010, she made a promise to her readers. She wrote that if she ever **published** a book, she'd fill a pool with marshmallows and jump in. It was a silly idea, but her goal was lofty. Veronica knew how difficult it is to get a book published. Only a fraction of manuscripts ever written are turned into books. But Veronica was hopeful. She never let herself think that her writing might not be good enough.

A few days later, Veronica's phone rang. It was her **agent**, Joanna Volpe. She had news. Big news. HarperCollins, a major publisher in New York, was interested in Veronica's book. This is the call all writers dream about.

Veronica knew what she had to do—jump into a pool of puffy white marshmallows.

The book, *Divergent*, would be the first in a **trilogy** of **dystopian** young adult (YA) novels. The series would go on to be one of the best-selling in YA history.

publish—to produce and distribute a book, magazine, newspaper, or any other printed material so that people can buy it

agent—someone who helps a writer find a publisher

trilogy—a series of three literary works that are related and follow the same story or theme

dystopian—a dangerous and bleak world likely created by a catastrophic event such as a virus outbreak or nuclear war

THE RISE OF YA

YA literature is a popular type of fiction today. A few decades ago, it didn't even exist. The first novel written for teens came out in 1942. It was a romance called *Seventeenth Summer* by Maureen Daly. Stories for 12 to 18 year olds weren't called "young adult" until the 1960s. By the early 2000s, YA authors such as Stephenie Meyer (*Twilight*), and Suzanne Collins (*The Hunger Games*) exploded onto bookshelves. Many adults read YA as well. Adults purchase nearly 55 percent of YA novels.

Veronica Roth

CHAPTER 2

"Boredom Is Not Allowed"

The young woman who went from wannabe author to YA superstar had come a long way. Veronica Roth was born on August 19, 1988. She grew up in a suburb of Chicago. Veronica had two older siblings.

When she was 5, Veronica's parents divorced. Her father worked far away. Veronica and her siblings had to rely on their mother, Barbara, for most things. Barbara's motto was "Boredom is not allowed." This helped Veronica develop her imagination. Instead of whining about having nothing to do, Veronica created pretend worlds in her backyard. Her mother did something else too. She read to Veronica every night. Surrounded by words, Veronica fell in love with books.

BOOK LOVER

Veronica didn't just read books. She devoured them. Some of them she read over and over. She read the entire Animorph and Ender's Game series multiple times. She had other favorites too. Veronica read **speculative fiction** such as *1984* by George Orwell and *A Wrinkle in Time* by Madeline L'Engle. In speculative fiction writers create worlds that are unlike the real world. These books would inspire Veronica's own writing.

✓ **FACT**

George Orwell's *1984* is one of the most famous dystopian novels ever written. It tells the story of Winston Smith as he rebels against a **totalitarian** government.

GEORGE ORWELL
1984

speculative fiction—a story with elements created out of imagination rather than real life

totalitarian—relating to a system in which the government has total control over the people

7

AN EARLY WRITER

When Veronica was in sixth grade, she began writing her own stories. According to her mother, Veronica "spent all of her free time writing." Veronica's stories contained many of the same elements as the books she loved reading—worlds with their own rules and brave main characters. Instead of creating adult **protagonists**, however, Veronica let younger characters take the lead.

"DRIVEN TO WRITE"

Veronica loved high school. She was a hard worker. She took advanced English, joined the government debate team, and sang in the choir. When she was a senior, Veronica won the National Council of Teachers of English Award in Writing, a prestigious honor. This was no surprise to her high school English teacher. Veronica stood out among other students. She not only worked hard, but she also noticed little details about people and things that she used to bring her stories to life. "There are a lot of kids who have talent," said her teacher, "but not the desire, and she has both. She's driven to write."

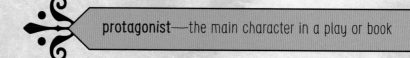
protagonist—the main character in a play or book

Veronica's early writing was similar to Divergent *in some ways.*

CHAPTER 3

Writing *Divergent*

After high school Veronica attended Carleton College in Minnesota. It was here that she got an idea for a new story.

The idea sprang from several experiences in Veronica's life. One occurred when she saw a billboard while driving. On the billboard was an image of somebody leaping off a building. The image captivated her. *Why would somebody do that?* Veronica wondered. At the time Veronica was also taking a psychology course about different kinds of fears. In one treatment she studied, people were exposed to their own fears. The idea was that exposure to fears would help reduce them.

Another influence was a lyric from the band Evanescence. When she heard the line, "fear is only in our minds, but it's taking over all the time," her story began to take shape. *What if someone had to prove her bravery*, Veronica wondered. Would she jump off a roof to do it? With all of these ideas floating around her mind, Veronica knew she was on to something.

Carleton College in Northfield, Minnesota

BECOMING FEARLESS

Slowly, what would become *Divergent* took shape. Veronica decided it would be about someone who had to not only confront her fears, but also become fearless. And they wouldn't be just any old fears. They would be the deepest and darkest fears imaginable. Things like leaping off buildings and away from trains thundering down the tracks. There would be secrets too. Secrets so big that one small slip would mean life or death.

Veronica's story centered on a feisty girl named Beatrice "Tris" Prior. Tris lives in a **post-apocalyptic** Chicago. In this future setting, the population is divided into five factions. Each faction represents a characteristic or virtue—Abnegation (selflessness), Dauntless (bravery), Erudite (intelligence), Candor (honesty), and Amity (peace). Tris doesn't fit into any of them. That makes her divergent.

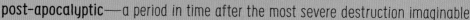
post-apocalyptic—a period in time after the most severe destruction imaginable

✔ FACT

Fans always ask what faction Veronica would choose. First, she claimed Dauntless. Who wouldn't want to think they were brave enough to jump off a train or rush down a zip line? But in the end, Abnegation won out. Veronica would rather have a peaceful life.

> Writing is really the only thing I've ever loved to do. The thought of being in a cubicle or doing a normal job made me want to cry, because it would take me away from this thing I wanted to do so much, so I think I tried because I was kind of desperate to do it.

—Veronica Roth, *Chicago Reader* interview, October 22, 2013

SECRET PROJECT

After a year at Carleton College, Veronica packed her bags. She transferred to Chicago's Northwestern University. There she began the school's creative writing program.

Although Veronica got the idea for *Divergent* in Minnesota, she didn't begin developing it until her sophomore year at Northwestern. Since the program concentrated on adult literature, Veronica thought her teachers wouldn't take her YA novel seriously. One professor even made a joke to Veronica about writing YA literature. Veronica was hurt. She kept *Divergent* as her own secret project.

OTHER WRITING

Veronica worked on other assignments during her time in college. She spent winter break of her senior year on her own writing. For 10 hours a day, Veronica wrote. The next month she spent revising. By February of 2010, Veronica knew it was time. She began the process of trying to get her first book published.

From Pitched to Published

In March 2010 Veronica attended the Midwest Writers Workshop conference in Indiana. She signed up to **pitch** her novel to a literary agent. It was a big opportunity. Aspiring authors rarely get to talk to an agent face-to-face. Veronica planned on presenting a story idea so captivating the agent would be dying to see more.

Instead of pitching *Divergent*, however, Veronica presented another novel she'd written. The agent liked her idea. She asked to see part of the manuscript. The agent liked what she read and asked for **revisions**. That was a great sign. It meant she was very interested. Veronica revised her manuscript. Then waited on pins and needles. Would the agent offer to represent her novel?

To Veronica's surprise, the agent rejected it. But there was good news too. The agent liked Veronica and her writing. She asked to see other manuscripts.

pitch—to present or advertise an idea or item

revision—the act of looking over again to correct and improve

Most authors go through several rounds of revisions before their book is published.

✔ FACT

Veronica lets music inspire her while she's writing. She listened to the album *Memento Mori* by the band Flyleaf while writing *Divergent*.

THE WAITING GAME

Submit another manuscript? Veronica could have been discouraged. But this setback only made her work harder. This time, she focused on her original secret YA novel, *Divergent*.

She pitched *Divergent* as the first book in a three-part series. Although she hadn't written the other two yet, she made a rough outline of the story. Veronica sent the **proposal** to the agent. Then she waited.

The agent loved it! After more revisions the agent agreed to represent Veronica. Her agent submitted *Divergent* to 12 publishers. Would Veronica's hard work pay off?

Four days later HarperCollins made an offer. It was unusually fast. Most authors wait weeks or months before they get a response. It was a sign HarperCollins thought Veronica's novel was going to be big.

FINDING A PUBLISHER

Finding a publisher isn't easy. After writers finish a manuscript, they send it to agents. Agents receive thousands of proposals a year. They reject most of them. When an agent reads a manuscript she thinks will be a good book, she sends it to publishers. Interested publishers make an offer to buy the book. The agent **negotiates** with the publisher until a final price is agreed upon.

ROTH DIVERGENT

ROTH ALLEGIANT

ROTH INSURGENT

When *HarperCollins* accepted *Divergent* for publication, Veronica agreed to also write two sequels, Allegiant *and* Insurgent.

proposal——an idea put forward for consideration

negotiate——to discuss a matter until reaching an agreement

THE CALL

Veronica was riding in an elevator when her agent called her with the good news. She darted out and ran down a dingy hallway into the area where the building kept its dumpsters. It was an awful place to receive such fantastic news. But Veronica didn't care. This news was so great that the place she heard it didn't matter.

When her agent dropped the bombshell, Veronica's legs went numb. She rushed back to her apartment and let the news settle in. It was a dream come true.

Now it was time for Veronica to keep the crazy promise she'd made on her blog. But when she actually thought of filling a pool with marshmallows, the whole thing seemed a bit unrealistic. A bathtub would be better. After tossing 42 bags of mini-marshmallows into her tub, a fully-clothed Veronica and her agent climbed in. They had a lot to celebrate.

Soon after the publication of *Divergent*, Veronica went on tour to promote the book, including this stop in Dublin, Ireland.

CHAPTER 5

Life as a Best Seller

Veronica's agent was right. *Divergent* was big! It debuted at number 6 on *The New York Times* Best Sellers list. A year later *Insurgent*, the second book in the series, debuted at number 1. The third book, *Allegiant*, met similar success in 2013.

Veronica was unprepared for the success and fame. Suddenly, the young author was going on book tours. She had to give interviews and speeches. "It was pretty shocking," said Veronica. She began having panic attacks. "People tell me, 'You don't look nervous.' But I'm like a duck on a pond: Under the surface, everything is churning away."

WRITING WOES

Writing the sequels had its challenges too. Veronica had a clear direction for *Divergent*. When she began writing *Insurgent*, Veronica dumped every idea she had onto the page. She admitted it was a "big mess." It took a lot of time to sort the good stuff from the bad.

Veronica giving an interview in 2015

ANXIETY DISORDERS

Doctors have diagnosed Veronica with an anxiety disorder. People with anxiety often worry and obsess more than what is considered normal. Veronica has struggled with anxiety since she was young. Bugs, heights, the public spotlight, and many other things trigger her anxiety. She says it's due to a chemical imbalance in her brain. Therapy has helped her deal with the panic attacks she suffered after the publication of *Divergent*.

MOVIE MAKING

Soon after the release of *Divergent*, a production company wanted to make it into a film. Although Veronica was uncomfortable with fame, she enjoyed the movie-making process. The movie version of *Divergent* was filmed in Chicago. Veronica was able to visit the set. "It was extremely weird to see famous actors act out scenes you've written," she said, "and then ... go home like it was any other day."

One day on the set, Veronica saw the giant tiled fighting arena she wrote about in the book. The sight brought her to tears. "It's like walking into my brain," she said.

Veronica didn't write the scripts for the movies. "I like writing," said Veronica. "I don't want to make movies." She consulted and offered feedback even though the producers didn't always take it. In the end Veronica learned to let go. "It's a little hard for an author to hand over a book to be adapted, but I've learned that the second the book comes out, it stops belonging to you. It belongs to the readers."

✔ FACT

Veronica makes a brief **cameo** in the *Divergent* film. She walks through the door at the top of the Hancock building right before Tris rides the zip line.

cameo—a brief appearance by a celebrity

Shailene Woodley and Theo James star in the movie versions of the Divergent books.

CHAPTER 6

What's Next?

Since becoming a best-selling author, Veronica continues to do what she's always done—write.

In the process she's learned not to respond to negative comments online. She has grown more accustomed to the spotlight. She's also met countless fans. Veronica says it's been special to talk to people who've read her book and hear their reactions. What would she like readers to take away from her books? "Questions," she says. "Questions about virtue and goodness. Not answers."

VIEWS ON WRITING

Veronica has adjusted her writing process too. Before *Divergent* nobody knew or cared what she wrote. She had a safe space free from others' opinions, expectations, and judgments. Now when she writes, she shuts out all that other stuff with a few mental tricks. She tells herself it's not the official document. She can trash it if she wants. "Mostly," says Veronica, "I just tell myself, 'Let it be bad. You can't edit a blank page.'"

Veronica signs autographs for fans during the *Divergent* movie premier in London.

> I believe that negative feedback, like many challenges and struggles in life, is essential for growth. I respect it, I consider it carefully, I let it shape my development as a writer, and then I get back to work.

—Veronica Roth, interview with goodreads.com, July 2014

THE NEXT SERIES

Veronica's latest two-book series will publish in 2017 and 2018. The story focuses on a boy's unlikely alliance with an enemy. Her publisher has compared the books to the film series Star Wars.

Veronica is taking her time and trusting her instincts. It's a process of writing, revising, and starting over if need be. When things don't work out, she steps away for a while to see things differently. Then she works on it again. She's learned to be more patient with herself—and her story. "It helps that I'm in love with this project," says Veronica. "That makes it a joy to work on."

Whatever comes next, Veronica will surely approach it with the same passion and determination that led to her first success.

WRITING ADVICE

Many aspiring writers ask Veronica for advice. She suggests patience—lots of it. Patience to learn about writing. Patience to polish a manuscript before making a hasty submission. Patience to learn the in's and out's of the publishing world. The favorite advice she received compared stories to backpacks. You should only pack what will get you to the end.

Glossary

agent (AY-juhnt)—someone who helps a writer find a publisher

cameo (KA-me-yoh)—a brief appearance by a celebrity

dystopian (diss-TOH-pee-uhn)—a dangerous and bleak world likely created by a catastrophic event such as a virus outbreak or nuclear war

negotiate (ni-GOH-shee-ate)—to discuss a matter until reaching an agreement

pitch (PICH)—to present or advertise an idea or item

post-apocalyptic (POHST-uh-PAHK-uh-lip-tik)—a period in time after the most severe destruction imaginable

proposal (pruh-POZE-uhl)—an idea put forward for consideration

protagonist (proh-TAG-uhn-ist)—the main character in a play or book

publish (PUHB-lish)—to produce and distribute a book, magazine, newspaper, or any other printed material so that people can buy it

revision (ree-VHIZ-shuhn)—the act of looking over again to correct and improve

speculative fiction (SPEK-yhul-uh-tiv FIK-shuhn)—a story with elements created out of imagination rather than real life

totalitarian (toe-tal-uh-TARE-ee-uhn)—relating to a system in which the government has total control over the people

trilogy (TRILL-uh-jee)—a series of three literary works that are related and follow the same story or theme

Read More

Anderson, Jennifer Joline. *Writing Fantastic Fiction.* Write This Way. Minneapolis: Lerner Publications, 2016.

Guillain, Charlotte. *What Is a Novel?* Connect with Text. Chicago: Heinemann Raintree, 2015.

Niver, Heather Moore. *Veronica Roth.* All About the Author. New York: Rosen Publishing, 2015.

Internet Sites

FactHound offers a safe, fun way to find Internet sites related to this book. All of the sites on FactHound have been researched by our staff.

Here's all you do:

Visit *www.facthound.com*

Type in this code: 9781515713272

Check out projects, games and lots more at
www.capstonekids.com

Critical Thinking Using the Common Core

1. Name one thing that inspired Veronica to write *Divergent*. (Key Idea and Details)

2. Reread the text on page 15. What if Veronica had focused on writing for adults instead of young adults? Do you think she ever would have written *Divergent*? Explain why or why not. (Integration of Knowledge and Ideas)

3. Reread the text on page 22 and study the photograph on page 23. What feelings do you think Veronica had while this photo was being taken? (Craft and Structure)

Index